Th
Within the Earth

The poetry of
Storm Faerywolf

Edited and with an introduction by
Chas Bogan

The Stars Within the Earth

Copyright ©2003 by Storm Faerywolf

Printed in U.S.A.

In darkness underneath the moon
The quiet forest sleeps
And hides the ancient mystery
Of that which lies beneath.

Down below the solid ground
The realm of all things known
By way of cave, or well, or mound
We journey toward the throne.

Past root and muck
And bone and shade
And place of crystal's birth
We seek the light within the dark
The stars within the earth.

They shine like jewels on velvet dark
And call us to our place
The stellar sphere
Is now drawn near
The paradox of space.

By foreign constellations led
To the palace of Her majesty.
Cthonic powers sleep below
Awaiting rediscovery.

The Faery mound that shrouds the gate
From prying eyes remains unseen
Except to those who's hearts yearn for
The kiss of Faery's Queen.

The King and Queen of Faeryland
Protect the secret power
Of divine spark within the land
Bringing consciousness to flower.

The bridge is us, that lies between
below and of above
And joining worlds unknown and seen
Our birthright formed in love.

INTRODUCTION

In the Western magical tradition, many have sought spiritual inspiration from above, associating starlight with enlightenment. Yet the stars can seem so distant, the divine so far from where we stand. Thank the Gods that we have poets, those who can lasso the stars and learn their secrets, who can reverse the act of Creation by turning light again into words. This is true magic.

You will find that this collection is full of magic. It manifests most apparently as rites, as liturgy, as directions for traversing other realms. In more abstract form it is the magic of transformation, such as is wrought by love. Love for both the mortal and the divine. Throughout this work there is alchemy at play, transmuting esoteric romance into passion that tangibly quickens the heart, and exposing the sacredness inherent in the profane. The message, in its myriad expressions, never fails to remind us that magic resides within us, just as the stars reside also inside the earth.

I have watched his work evolve, doing so in directions I would never have ventured. For over a decade (at the time of this writing), I have been stirred by the magic of Storm's words, and, I hope, inspired him in turn. He has shared with me many dreams and visions that remain intimate between us, while others he has shared with the world, such as inspired him to take the name 'Faerywolf.' These poems are something in-between; magic released into the world for all to experience, and for every heart to have personal intimacy with.

Chas Bogan
Dec. 16, 2003

"Invoking the BlackHeart"
©2003

1: Stars of Love

Always You
For Chas

You are the one I give my life to
The one I come to
I one I feel
Inside of my heart between each beat
Each spasm of this pumping muscle an invocation
Of my love for you.
Oh, how we've fought
Over the years
Our egos clashing like swords in a duel
But when I am wounded it is you who tends to me
It is you who heals me
It is you
Always you

Only a Whisper

My heart has opened to you,
and there's no denying it.
For you I yearn, for you I tremble.
Our time is short and so my heart
speaks its truth with rare abandon.

I have recognized you...
from across time's ocean
and the river of forgetfulness.
I have searched for you in the land of dreams,
and found you now in the world of waking.
Fate has brought us together once more.
My heart knows yours.

They have embraced in intimate communion
(these liquid lights that merge as one)
Both are changed now, both made deeper:
There is a piece of your soul forever in my heart.
I will keep it safe until forever comes.

A part of me is always with you,
returning to my love-sick heart only when
I drink of the wine of your sweetest kiss.
(O let me be drunk on it!)

I look into your eyes and am changed.
No longer of the world outside,
my life is only love's devotion.
My beloved, my beautiful boy,
I sit at your feet and muse these words,
in the hopes that behind them you will find
the faintest whisper of my love for you.

Only a whisper, soft on the breeze
(for what do words know of love?)

I ask you to forgive my clumsy writ,
and look to the power that it invokes.

Breathe it in, this is my love.
Let it caress you,
as I ache to do.
Let it fill your heart,
as you have filled mine.
Rejoice in it,
as I do.

My heart has opened to you,
and there's no denying it.
For you I yearn, for you I tremble.
Our time is short and so my heart
speaks its truth with rare abandon.

Dance of the Beloved

You are the flame,
that burns in my heart.
you are the sweet water,
that quenches my thirst.
you are the beloved,
and I hold you up for all to see.
dance with me, my beloved,
dance and share in the revelry
of the stars and the planets
spinning into drunken bliss,
as I look into your eyes,
and see none other than the face of desire.

a little dream

thinking of you...
soon to be dreaming of you.
even while you are away,
you dwell in my heart.

Beneath the Words, Lies Love

Some things are deeper,
than words can allow.

Some things lie below
the surface of our knowing.

I reject all words, all knowing.
They do not reflect
the depths of my heart.
Sometimes with love comes
the pain of two hearts
beating out of unison.

Wait!

Their time will come,
their cycles will be realized,
and ours will too.

Hang on,
and wait with me,
and listen to our two hearts beating.

The Prayer in the Kiss

kiss upon kiss,
fueling the fires of passion,
the gateway to the beloved opens,
in the surrender of the will to the body,
which is the temple of every god known
and so my prayer is made:
that we find ourselves in each other's arms,
soon.

The Dreaming Mystery

We walk within the Dreaming Lands,
to look upon the face of love.
The Ancient Gods upon our breath,
our beating hearts the Mothers' Drum.

We dance in the spiraled rhythm of knowing:
(What was pain before is now our strength.)
We climb to the zenith of our understanding,
to cast our gaze across the great expanse.

Where does our love now choose to lead us?
How can we know what is to be???
We trust the strangeness of our hearts,
and move to brush against the Mystery.

Awakened are we, within this dream.
Only now before us the path is seen.
The light of our hearts made strong shines brightly,
and guides us, eternally, toward the infinite.

Call to the Heavenly Lover

Heavenly Lover,
who comes at night to caress my ears with silken whispers,
who sends dreams that fill my heart with precious longing,
I call to you.
Quench my thirst for you, for I am parched,
Your sweet nectar is my only solace
here in the desert of my soul.

Arise within me on the waves of my own pleasure,
that I may do your work here upon the Earth.
Swell up within me like the waters of the ocean and make your will
be known
that all may be healed of the false fissure in the spiritual flesh.
Make Holy the pleasures of the body's wisdom,
Make known the secret passion of the heart,
that is the key to the Mystery.

Remember the Light in your Eyes

There is a light in your eyes,
Shining from the fire in your heart.
Others have been lured by it,
from their dreamless sleep,
to rise and look upon your face,
to be guided to the place of true existence.
Can you see it?
Remember your origin!
From amongst the stars you were born.
You are the willing vessel of the Gods,
compassion poured upon the earth
like rain that leaves the parched soil
gasping with ecstasy.
Close your eyes,
and let your light shine inward.
Do you remember now?
How the laughter and tears
brought you into this moment...
How the pain was but a bridge
to the realm of the infinite?
Take a deep breath,
and remember.
Remember how we used to dance,
in circles on the grass until we collapsed,
giggling like children (I guess we were, then).
I remember... I am reminded by the light in your eyes.

All the love my heart can hold

All the love my heart can hold
is for you, my dear.
Look for it in my eyes when I gaze into your soul.
Feel it in my kiss when I take you away from the mundane world.
And mirror it back, I beg, for you lift me into the heavens.
I shine with the love you give to me.
My heart is full of it.

You Who are my Star

The thought of you,
warms and gives me light.
You who are my star,
you who are my world,
are always with me,
here in my heart.

My dreams are now only of you,
I long only for your touch,
Everything else pales in comparison.

Am I being unfair
to those around me?
I see them talking but I can't hear their words.
Everything that was important to me once now seems trivial.
Just kiss me and everything will be right in the world.

Show me your beauty,
your tremendous beauty.
Let it shine so that even the sun and the moon will be jealous of
your splendor,
and everything will be right in the world.

I sit alone,
yet I am not alone,
for my heart is filled with your light,
and all those around me know that it is your light that shines from
my chest,
and so they know the truth of it:
I am a better person because I love you.

Untitled

Can I just weep now,
and get it over with?
I feel I can stand the tears,
now with my joy to protect me.

I am slain by the Divine,
I the moth and you the flame,
and my love for you the sword
that pierces my precious flesh,
as I bleed in ecstasy.

There is a piece of my soul
that is only with me when you are near.
I look into your eyes and see the faces
of princes and beggars, and lovers and saints,
and everything in between,
and I know in my heart that we have been together
for eternity.
But not now.

Savoring the Surprised Heart

You were the one who surprised my heart.
I didn't know that I was searching for you...
Yet now my heart has found yours.
And as you travel far away,
I remember looking into your eyes and getting lost...
All day those eyes would haunt me
until I spoke to you and told you
how much you meant to me.
I remember...
Touching your body was a delight that I savor
in my mind where it lasts forever.
The taste of your kiss sent me swirling,
swirling,
into liquid bliss covered with light,
shimmering from the heart of love.
Remember me, is all I ask,
and think of me fondly when you do.
Remember the short time we had together
and know that you are loved.
And if the Fates decide we shall love again,
I'll rejoice in their wisdom and follow my heart.
And if they decide that our paths no longer cross,
I'll remember you fondly, and in my heart
will keep you
forever.

"The Love of Gods and Men"
©2004

The Open Heart

Tender One,
Golden One,
Arouser of the flame,
I offer myself to you,
My heart the vessel of your love,
overflowing on the earth.

Smooth One,
Silken One,
Seducer of the flesh,
The feeling we share
when our eyes meet
is the invitation to spirit
to flow like water between us,
and it washes away all doubt in my mind,
all fear shrinks back at your beautiful light,
and I join the faery dance,
in sweet abandon.

But for your light to illumine
the most hidden parts of my soul
means that I stand naked before you
and so I tremble.
The fear I thought conquered returns,
from a place deep within my body,
so deep that no one knew it was there,
and now I sit alone thinking on your face,
your touch,
your kiss,
and I weep for those things lost.

But then I remember the gift that you brought me,
and how real my love is
and it makes a difference.
how you reached inside me and
reminded me of my spirit.

I give thanks to you.
and surrender to the will of spirit touched by flesh
and bathed in song.
Between us is the circle of all that is.
How could I not have noticed its absence before?

My head is spinning.
Everything that I once knew is gone from here,
There is only this love that matters,
flowing through my heart so strong that I fear it shall burst into fire,
and consume all that I hold dear:
my boundaries and my fears.

Sweet liberator,
Warrior of the soul,
Shall we dance and forget about the complexities of our situation?
Shall we feast on each others gaze while waiting for that moment we
know will come
all too soon?
My skin is on fire at the thought of your touch,
at the thought of that moment when God fills our souls with the
truth (once forbidden)
I can only exist,
and breathe,
and wait,
and see what life holds for us.
I will not hold on
for I know too well that ancient curse.

Clear headed now I rise up and remember the moment
when I first felt your love
and it will sustain me
until the end of my days.

The Flight of the Fall

I have abandoned all that I have known,
in favor of you.
I have denounced all that I have stood for,
to stand in your presence.
I have relished that which was forbidden to me,
in the taste of your lips.
Through you I know union and understand
the great pattern of creation.
My heart takes flight and with it my body,
trembling at first then calm,
soars above the earth to take in Her splendor.
The seasons change, yet I am unchanged.
In the face of love
I am eternal.
This holy accident of the spirit,
this fall,
this descent into the pleasures of the body
has redeemed my soul and made me a resident
of the shining country of bliss.
I renounce my former homeland for it is false,
and make forever my home in your love.
I am made the Fool,
and so I dance ecstatic,
frenzied, and fierce,
the rhythm of my body is the pulsing of the heart of God.
My flesh is God's body sent to touch the very pleasure of you.
In this love I am washed clean,
the burden of logic has been lifted.
This sweet madness has freed me
and my soul joins my body and my heart,
on the wings of an angel,
spiraling into the infinite.

The Sense of my Love

Do you feel my love?
It is pouring from the vessel of my heart.
Do you hear my love?
It is singing on the breezes of the night.

Do you see my love?
It is shining like a guiding star.
Do you taste my love?
It is sweet nectar sent from the gods of ecstasy.

My love is the force that created the heavens,
Waves of it pulse from me in my blood,
Sending the message of the Divine into all the worlds,
Caressing the beloved.

This passion that fills me
brings with it the death of logical illusion.
My mind betrays my heart, and so I will not think.
I will only feel this, my love, and let the heavens dance in my heart.
I am out of my head. I am mad with it.

A Beautiful Memory

When I look at the moon I still dream of you.
(It was you who illumined my heart.)
Thank you for showing me the way
to the river of bliss,
that washes away all pain.
I was renewed with the promise of you.
I was made whole again.
And now on my way I walk
into another place
with my memories as precious treasures.
Your face in my mind lifts me up to the holiest of holies.
A dream, but one that will stay inside me
forever.

"In the Presence of the BlueGod"
©2001

2: Stars of Prayer

A Prayer to Dian y Glas

Blue God,
Laughing God,
Dancer at the Well of Springtime,
Spread your peacock fan and make
Music with your steps.

Lord of many feathered eyes
Looking into many places,
Let us see ourselves through you,
And in you see ourselves reflected,
And by this vision come to know
Each other through the dance.

And through those eyes, those many eyes,
Touching tender in the dark,
A sweet caress of liquid light,
Flash of pleasure now arise:
The serpent from the Well.

Shining One, Silken One, He of many touches,
Enrapture me in your embrace,
And through our ecstasy create
Again, my love, the earth and heavens,
Made anew each moonlit night,
And send me smiling softly dreaming,
Into the lands of bliss.

Prayer to the All-Mother

Holy Mother,
Womb of the Universe,
Creator of destiny,
Eater of time,
All exists within your body,
Your power flows within my veins.

The God of the World

In Darkness was the world first born,
From the ink-black womb of Mother Night,
Now see the Darkness so adorned,
with the jewels of cosmic light.

Sapphire skin and eyes full of lust
the feathers of peacocks are swathed on His skin
Seduction His secret, His passions a must
He beckons now to you; will you let Him in?

He walks in the garden; in the mirror he gazes
Of She who is Goddess and Mother of All
Transfixed by His beauty he yearns for the praises
Of souls of humanity, His jewels of the fall.

Some call Him the Devil; we call him our God
The soul of our spirit and redeemer as well
This earthen angel fills heavens with thunder
His tears have extinguished the fires of hell.

A Creation Story

Before the beginning of all things was She
Who moved in the blackness of infinity
Before time and reason
Before shade and form
She gazed into the mirror of space, curved and black
and saw Her own reflection smiling back.

Aroused by Her vision of Herself
She made love
To Her own reflection She made love
And the Universe was born
On the waves of Her pleasure
The waves of all Creation.

This was the first light
That divided the primal dark
That enabled the divine spark
That brought forth all life.

Moving then away from She
Who is the Starry Mother of All
The reflection takes on new form, Behold!
The laughing God of love.

Walking in the peaceful Garden
With Her child, son, and lover
He yearns for those to see His beauty
The souls of women and of men.

"Think well on this", the Goddess says
"For if this is done there is a price.
Your head will remain in heaven, true

36

But your feet will be caught in hell."

"But I love them", said the gentle God
"I want them for my precious jewels"
And seeing the love held in His eyes
The Goddess moved to grant His wish.

So the Goddess spoke,
"Io Evohe. Blessed be!"
And amidst great lightning and thunder
thus were born the souls on Earth.

Circle Dance

I
see a hill
in the dark
of the night

And the glow
of the moon
shining down
with silvered light

So shall we
gather here
in a circle
in Her name
and we dance
from our hearts
and will never
be the same

Hear the beat
of the drum
as the Earth's
beating heart
and then know
beyond a doubt
that we can never
be apart

for the truth
lies in the stars
is in the grasses
and the stones
It's in the birds
and in the foxes
and the spiders
and the bones

So if you
were then to listen
to the deepest
mysteries
sit there quiet
wrapped in moonlight
look around
and there you'll see

For the wind
and the clouds
and the bats
and the moths
dance
a little dance
in the darkness
for Her love.

In Darkness Mirror

There is a light
In the darkness of night
The Radiant Jewel
The giver of sight.

She spirals above in Her cosmic cacophony
As galaxies whirling proclaim Her great majesty.
She shines from above in Her pale lunar symphony
To shine down below on terrestrial destiny.

Shine down below...
> *Shine down below...*

The Star-Child sleeps in the earth down below.

Into the darkened womb of Earth
The place where meets both death and birth
A light, forgotten, now rests in its place
Dressed in the darkness of matter and space.

A light from the darkness! Arise from your place!

He stretches his feathers
He lifts up His face
He dances in spirals
And allures Her embrace.
Two lights in the darkness,
Two sides of Her face.

Their love is eternal
To which they belong.
Love and Beloved,
The mirror! The song!

The blackness of midnight
The promise of dawn.

Reveal the secret, the veil is drawn!

Nine points the star that forms the Gate
And seven tumblers in the lock
By five the key to earthly space
Her Triple Will in life we walk.
The Two have melted now together
And One is fleeing from the shade
Into the darkness of oblivion
And here we see our prayer is made.

Into the face of darkness mirror
We clear our thoughts and cast our gaze,
As Ana the Black will make things clearer,
At least when comes our end of days.

River of Moonlight

You yearn for the mysteries
of Melek Taus
the Peacock Lord,
the seducer of souls.
The angel of earth
who fell down from heaven
who brought down the stars
who taught us the Art.
He holds in his eyes the fire of life
Stolen from heaven,
The flame of the soul.
With serpentine dances
and dark longing glances
He lures you out in the cloak of the night
The serpents will rise and the hush that will follow
That leads to abandon
That leads to their realm.
To taste wicked pleasures (His voice is like music)
To love earthen treasures (His touch is like silk)
To drink and get drunk on a river of moonlight
And sing, both together, with hearts now as one
As white fire flows from the passionate one.
Drink deep of the God of the flesh,
Drink deep of the God of the soul,
Drink deep of His passion,
And make it your own.

Light-Bringer

From the womb of Mother Night,
The first star born to bring forth light
Falls to earth on angel's wings,
Watching, waiting, laughing, singing,
Strutting in His peacock dance,
Calling down the wild-eyed trance,
Shaking heaven, tearing hell,
The serpent rises from the well.

The Love of Kings

Two lovers in a sacred ring
The Kings of Holly and of Oak
Dancing dervish 'round the sun
Desire whirling, hot and wild.

As passion swells with quickened blood
As summer leads to longing
The solstice sun shall mark the time
When Oak shall bow to Holly.

Into their eyes the light of love
Into their hearts sweet passions' flame
Into their kiss a fevered moment
In their embrace, Her Holy Name.

By seed and bud, by fruit and flower,
That all may spiral through rebirth
With milk of moon they spill their power
Their love is poured upon the earth.

As the chill moves on the wind
That heralds winter's cloak
The solstice sun shall mark the time
When Holly bows to Oak.

Into their eyes the light of love
Into their hearts sweet passions' flame
Into their kiss a fevered moment
In their embrace, Her Holy Name.

Two lovers in a sacred ring
The Kings of Holly and of Oak
Dancing dervish 'round the sun
Desire whirling, hot and wild.

Dance of the Blue God

The Blue God has come to me,
today as a person.
Dian y Glas has come to me,
clothed in the flesh.
So sweet to the touch,
So silken.
To look upon you is to see the face of God.
My heart is enraptured at the smallest glance.

Fill me up with your wine,
For I am the cup.
Pierce me with your love,
For you are the sword.
Sweet boy,
Let us dance together in the dance of love,
which is the dance of creation,
and destruction,
and rebirth.

Toward renewal we spin,
as the serpent rises,
from the depths of the well in the springtime of the soul.
The caress of your eyelashes,
dripping with ecstasy,
is the fluttering of your painted fan.
The words from your heart,
are the melodies of your silver flute,
and I am intoxicated by your drunken tune.
Arise! And come to me, O Beautiful One.
Arise! And come. Arise, and come.
Arise! And come to me, O Sensual One,
and dance through the passion in my soul.

Narcissus

From the east in springtime walking,
toward the brook with shade of tree,
Narcissus sits while calmly looking,
into the waters bubbling free.

Down below this place of motion,
into the darkened place of rest,
exists the secrets of all loving,
Narcissus moves to see them best.

A deeper gaze into the waters,
reveals longing in the heart,
a love surpassing all known beauty,
Narcissus pierced by Cupid's dart.

An overflowing heart with love,
that spills into a crystal stream,
reflects upon the moving waters,
and calls for union in the deep.

Closer to the mirrored waters,
Narcissus leans to catch a glimpse,
of the one who beckons softly,
from underneath with parted lips.

Moving forward for the kiss,
Narcissus takes his final breath,
and dives into the icy waters,
to meet with secrets beyond death.

Delving into dreams below,
discovery of what was torn apart,
of self and knowing, self and love,
and union now with this, his heart.

Don't weep for him, our passing hero,
true his time on earth did pass,
but through his heart made whole he conquered,
reborn into the Shining Lands.

Passing

In loss, tears flow into a river,
flowing outward into the western lands,
like a beacon to those who have departed
and they know:
they are loved and are remembered.
Open now is the gate of sorrow,
Let tears fall like rain to cleanse the soul.
Grief is the bridge to rebirth.
So shriek at the heavens and mourn your loss,
tear at your clothes and sob into the Mothers' breast.
Then take your love and wear it proudly,
let it shine amongst the heavens like a star,
guiding souls to the land of rest.

Prayer of the Mystery

I pray to the Holy Mother of Night
whose stellar fire illumines the dark
Reveal the secret path to truth
that within us all exists your spark.

May all three souls be aligned within us
and may we see through veil drawn
the precious jewel of ruby's kiss
and know that it is safe from harm.

Watchers from the brink of dawn
From noon, from dusk, from midnight's grasp
Encircle sacred secret lore
That dishonor shall not pass.

By silence I shall keep my Oath
By daring feat of trust and love
By my own true will, I know the truth
As is below, so is above.

You Ask, "What is Faerie?"

It is the rolling of the wave
the fire that has quickened
the breath that has inspired
the vessel that is pure
the starlight in the daytime
the vision turned to dreamtime
the power from beyond time
the bardic songs of yore.

Holy Mother, in you we live
breathe, move, and have our being
To You we pray
we are your children
To You we pray
We are Yourself.

The Forgotten Ancestors

They are without name and number
without face or memory
Or shade
Or form
But still they live
As hungry ghosts
feeding on the crusts of bread
And the kindness of strangers.
But they are not unknown to us
Not completely.
The men and women of secret passions
The man who wore a dress and was arrested
Taken away in a wagon of queers
The woman
With hair cut short and wearing slacks
Like any gentleman on the town.
They are still here with us
Wandering lost.
Wander no more for we remember
Though we know not your names, we remember!
You who lived your lives on your own terms
Who broke the molds and lived
And suffered
And laughed,
And died
All in the name of love.
We honor you.

Invocation of The Holy Cock

Scarlet scepter,
shaft of life,
rising and falling, this pillar of flesh,
arousal of passion,
the flame of desire,
bears witness now to the triumph of pleasure!

This hunger,
This Hunger,
This burning desire,
fed only by the stiffened flesh,
of animal lust and Divine attraction
Leads us as seekers with bended knee
into the religion of the ancient God.

Where we worship,
with parted lips,
our mouths agape with wild tongue,
ready to receive communion
with the Lord of the Sacred Fuck.

Nectar rains from the Lord above,
we struggle to taste the flavor of bliss.
Rain down on our faces and renew our spirits.
We drink of the essence and nourish our souls.

Anoint our skin with the holy balm,
The pungent scent that first enraptures
Then claims as servants those who are marked
By thickened fragrance of lust and spunk,
The baptismal of flesh made sacred.

Our heads begin to sway and swim,
We who are drunk on the milk of God,
Our mouths the cup that overflows,
His love onto the earth.

There is such beauty in the seed that is spilled in the name of lust.
Through this we are all made God.
Through this our bodies are made Holy.

The Black Heart of Innocence

In the beginning of all life
Before the soul is caught and snared
There exists a point of light
Hiding in the darkness there.

Some fear the dark, the ink-black night
That clothes our precious earth
Still others know it is a gift
And ours by right of birth.

How pure the souls of animals
And wild children living free
Singing loud and smiling wide
A natural life allowed to be.

To this precious state of life
Our path we must return
And abandon chains of social strife
To this end we shall learn.

Iron star within my blood
Souls of three aligned within
Star of pearl connects us all
To our undistorted origin.

Many names have been attached
To this feeling and this sense
Of unrestrained expression called
The Black Heart of Innocence.

Invocation of the Queer Ones

From the Lavender Lands, and the space in between,
From the cracks in the world, in the order of things,
We summon the Queer Ones, the fount of our love,
To rise from below and descend from above,
To bridge now the gap that exists in our hearts,
To heal the pain that has torn us apart.
Bring us your laughter and lend us your song.
Join in the struggle endured for so long,
That we now might taste of the water of life,
And be free from the curse
that has caused us such strife.
Let us remember our power and place
Of our home from the stars, in the sweet ones embrace,
To reclaim now the ancient blessing once given,
from the Goddess of Earth, the Goddess of Heaven:
For ours is the wisdom of moon and of earth,
We stand at the gate between death and of birth.
As the fathers of beauty, as the mothers of souls,
we are healers of spirit, and we walk between worlds.

Prayer to the Old Gods

Sacred Mother, Maiden, Crone
Holy Brother, Son and Lover
I am marked by Mystery's kiss
By Triple Will I am Thrice thine.

I sing of Your stories, I speak Your great names
I dance in a circle and madness descends
I drink of the Power that flows from Your river
the currents that take me to sanity's end.

The smooth edge of space, that curved and black mirror,
where the laws of humanity can ne'er reside
Conjures the Seven and then draws Them nearer
to again walk upon this green earth filled with life.

From the dark and silver egg
the firstborn Twins are born with lust
Seductive softness is Their name
And fall into Their spell we must

Arousal of innocence, the bud on the stem
that opens, so softly, in pale early sun
That possesses a beauty as such beyond knowing
To proclaim morning's majesty with flower and thorn.

White One! Blue One!

Your breasts are soft hillsides; Your eyes are as pools
Your sex is a cave, and a well, and a geyser
Your skin petal soft to the touch makes me drunken
Your lust is the power that brings seeds to flower

We hear you on the wings of doves
We smell you in the scent of flowers
We feel you in the cool spring breeze
We see you in the eyes of love.

The Twins, they do move and they take on the pallor
of pale moon light and of bright summer's peak
Pregnant with promise, erect with their vigor
As Mother and Horned One together we seek

Mother Green, and Red, and Black!
Lover, Garland swathed and Golden!

By Moon and by Ocean, By stag and by wren
Cool rain is your kiss, warm sun is your treasure
Your perfume the scent of sweet blossoms in daytime
And soft dripping pollen your spent summer's pleasure.

We hear you in the crack of fire
We smell you in the musk of heat
We feel you in the thrust of rutting
We see you in the golden wheat.

As summer skies shall soon give way
to winter's touch and turn to gray
as so we too in turn must meet
the scythe of She whose face we seek.

Rending thunder, howling shriek
splintered bone for flesh is weak
the pain and horror as death takes hold
the final stare that's now grown cold.

Dark One! Black One! Wise One! Mad One!

Silent wisdom guards the gate,
to the final mystery
The Royal Darkness who shall preside
over the end of history.

Ancient Mother, singing sweetly
Lustful harlot, scarlet kiss
within your womb are things made holy
the black of madness is your bliss.

We hear you in the voice of toads
We smell you in the damp of earth
We feel you in caress of rain
We see you in the pangs of birth

Mother Darksome and Divine
Let thy worshipers rejoice
For thou art virgin ever new
and all of life speaks with your voice.

The Renewal of Truth

From the ashes there shall rise anew
a hopeful phoenix
weathered, wizened, with skin like leather
shining eyes taking in the dawn
sharp claws grasping
the sword of truth
O warrior!
Thou art reborn!
O lover!
Once again we shall know your touch.

The Faerie Tale

Down into the rabbit hole,
and up into the twister,
here we find the rabbit white,
as a house falls on the sister
of the wicked queen of hearts,
who in a tirade strikes
and sends her monkeys flying to
imprison little tikes.

Chant the chant and sing the song,
the towered princess casts her hair
to charming princes, frogs and all
the fairy's gift is deep in there.

To ancient castles we must ride
Through magic forests alive with laughter
to challenge darkness and fulfil the promise:
"they lived happily ever after"

A Wicked Witch, an evil Queen,
a grotesque monster for good measure
a shining knight, a hero's fight,
a kiss, a kingdom, a new found treasure.

The children freed in their hour of need
the evil spell is broken
all goes well, and the bad guys go to hell
and heaven awaits us in slumber.

We know well the stories and tell of their tales,
how the dragons of discord were vanquished and sold
yet I weep for their passing and hope they are hiding
for their presence lends magick
not oft known in this world.

So I look for the Old Gods, the beasts, and the fairies,
I speak of their names and their sigils I mime
their stories, perpetually grand invocations
are secrets preserved in the midst of a rhyme

And what did we learn down the yellow brick road?
And what did Alice really find down that hole?

Well...

It's a shaman's journey if ever I saw one,
and I ought to know cause I'm continually on one
and from what I've learned,
what I've seen,
what I've read
Better bring your own slippers,
Now good night, go to bed.

The Lustful Dark

In the darkness just beyond my sight
A lusty satyr waits within the night.
The dark, His sweet caress upon my skin
A trembling quiver begs to let Him in.
"Fear not, sweet Lover", the words upon His lips
flow like wine unto me in His kiss
I drink them in with passion and design
For I know their secret power is Divine.
My hardened sex my wand upheld in praise
Reveals the inner flame now set ablaze.
The full moon casts Her silver pallor down
To Her Son who wears the earthly crown
Who stalks this moment just beyond my reach
I want to learn and He's about to teach.
Satin strokes and several wicked pleasures
Forbidden kisses, and forbidden treasure
The scent of man and the touch of flesh
Of bodies writhing, tangled, wet, enmeshed.
It sends me spinning breathing in His power
I am His prey and soon He will devour
I feel Him inside my body and my soul
With Him inside I know that I am whole.
His power is like fire in my veins
I beg with thrusting hips he shall remain
With rutting madness and with wild tongue
A song of primal pleasure now is sung
As darkness calls the mystery to arise
the howling wolf then drowns our lusty cries.
With white hot bursts of ivory fire's seed
Flowing down like milk to fill the need
An offering of my pleasure and delight
To He Who Is Seducer of the Night.

The Power of Blue

The Blue Fairy plays His silver flute
And in my dreams He roams
Above the skies He guides me high
Wearing stars as precious stones.

Lady Blue, Her Queenly form
Dressed in jewels and silken mime
From deep beneath the earthen mound
Her eyes as black as midnight's chime.

The open book reveals to me
My own skin stained with woad
And then I know I'm one of yours
You've come to take me home.

Faery ways and Faerie blood
Fairy wings and Feri power
I accept thy sovereign gifts and then
Bestow them on another.

Will you find your soul of blue?
It's living there deep within
And waiting now to guide you to
What you have always been.

The Old Man in the South

In the place of noonday heat I walk,
To seek the silence that lives there.
For silence is the treasure of
The sacred fire that burns there.

Into the desert I have stepped
sand hot upon my feet
And rings of fire appear and not
The bitter gift of heat.

Beyond the rocks, the hardened clay
Baked by ever-summer's sun
The Old Man works his craft all day
For the silence he was won.

I pull up a stone and sit at his feet
and ne'er a word is spoken
and in reverent silence I learn of the art
of the Will that can never be broken.

The fire it burns in the belly, down deep
So that breathing shall cause it to ember
A throb and thrum glow, a vibration you'll know
That shall awaken it from its own slumber.

The flame it fills the body entire
So that your every inch is on fire
And your life is consumed, and refined, and resumed
Transformed by a focused desire.

All flames are one, the saying goes,
The hearth, the star, the Divine spark,
You breathe them in, and you breathe them out
So that sitting alone, you are empty and dark.

Breathing...
                      Heat upon your breath
Breathing...
                      hotness on your skin
Breathing...
                      flames around you glow
Breathing...
                      The burning flame that is within

Burning... burning...
Turning... turning...
Revealing, revealing...
Silence.

The Kiss of Dian y Glas

From the stars the boy was born,
shining blue with longing eyes,
Soft as many petaled rose,
He lifts my soul into the skies.

Beyond the ego's iron gate,
beyond the stars and moon,
into Dian y Glas' kiss,
that's where you'll find me soon.

My head is spinning, my lips do part,
I fall into a drunken haze,
For into Faery I have stumbled,
and here now I shall spend my days.

My body sings with silken pleasure,
My mind filled only with delight,
My triple soul enraptured with
the power of His softened might.

Now for the bed, the serpent rises,
stretches upwards for his kiss,
a flashing tongue of silver satin
a holy river made of bliss.

The Child in the Paper Dress

The child in the paper dress
With dirty streaks across her face
Walks barefoot in the grass and plays
With the butterflies.

The child in the paper dress
Grinning madly at the sun
Scratches wildly in the dirt
As snakes writhe in her hair.

The child in the paper dress
Dances fast around the well
Laughing loud and skipping high
She struts with innocence and lust.

The child in the paper dress
With teeth bared and a snarl
Becomes a beast ferocious quick
Then hums a sing-song tune.

The child in the paper dress
So tattered and so white
As old as stones, as young as fate
Her red hair wild, as is her gaze.

The child in the paper dress
With dirty streaks across her face
Walks barefoot in the grass and plays
With the butterflies.

The Angels Stand Just There

There is a silent shriek
Electric lightning thunderclaps
Rain against the window glass
Night outside my room

Standing at the edge of dreams
Beneath my feet they shine
eyes cold and beautiful
bathed in storm and moon

Golden skin and golden hair
He looks soft enough to kiss
And she, younger, stands just there
Inhuman eyes that draw me near

I rise
Against my own free will
A pit in my stomach
Aches as if poisoned.

I am drawn,
Against my trembling fear
A sound in my ears
Deafens all reason.

I cannot move
I cannot speak
My soul is snared
My power faltered
Seized by fear and gripped with malice
A trap is set and I am captured

Breathing slow and breathing deep
Arise thy spark!
Arise and conquer!
Fire deep within the soul
Defend the boundaries of thy master!

I find my voice; I find my power
I hum my spell
I sing my tune
The star of nature is my shield
Into this realm am firmly rooted.

Emblazoned sigil in my mind
My throaty drone empowers thee
To cast false angels to the wind
As I WILL, So MOTE IT BE!

The spell is broken
My guests depart
I fall down exhausted
I sleep without dream.

The Mushroom

The faery atop the mushroom
guards its magick flesh
she beckons you to taste its fruit
filled with dreams and poison
a bitter taste within your mouth
the sound of rushing wind
your head is filled with stars and wonder
your soul is filled with music.
Naked you dance atop a hill
With fireflies in your hair
Dance within the faery ring
And court the madness that it brings
So that you may see what is unseen
The hidden powers
Of life.

The Fear and the Knife

Fear of death creeps over me
Time and time again
Black slicing madness of eternity
A tremor in my brain.

The end of reason
The end of thought
The end of feeling
The end of form
Calling from across the Void
Calling me back home.

Greeted at the gate by He
Who over darkness rules
I shed the garments of my life
My soul a shining jewel.

My fear I give
I now release
It's grip upon my throat
And offer it up to She who is
Mysterious and remote.

Clad in black, Her silk fine hair
In strands of pearl and white
A silver sickle stained with blood
Reflects the full moon's light.

The gate is opened wide and then
I see beyond my life
And know beyond the shades of doubt
The gift of Ana's knife.

Green Goddess

New, you come, to sunlight's kiss
Your verdant pallor
So strong in the hour
Of eastern rise of fire's gift
O Gracious Goddess, drink it in!

Strands of amber, gold, and violet
Wearing crystals in your crown
You give the sight by way of breath
Your way is of the open heart.

Through smoke filled room
And drunken haze
I come to you,
Priestess! Teacher!
Bring me to the way of peace
Through soul of laughter I am your priest.

Song of the White Goddess

On waves of my breath
The white fire comes
That enters my body
That enters my mind.
The flame of her presence
The power of moonlight
The roaring of firelight
The calm in the storm
The color of crystal
The fountain of music
The tower of ivory
Her power reborn.

She sings in Her glory
She dances a dream
In spirals of living, and dying again
The earth is Her body
And nature Her Will
The seasons Her passion and pleasure and thrill.

Her language is spoken on wind through the trees
Her favor is granted to those who can know
That all issues forth from her womb made of darkness
We are part of Her spiral,
As above so below.

In stillness breathe deeply
While sitting and calm
And quietly listen to your voice within
For your voice is Her voice
She lives there inside you
Waiting to show you what you've always been.

The Watchers of the World

The morning sun that steps upon the clouds,
is the great herald that speaks your name.
Dancing proud across the sky,
your eyes are stars, your touch is golden.
We sing together through our breath,
the sacred spiral made manifest.

Sharpness is the tongue of flame,
that slices through the great illusion.
A sword of strength that steadily rises
to greet the sun of summer's skies,
finds its place and turns the wheel
that all may live and grow and die.

Flowing twilight, sinking dream,
rising from the depths below,
where light and dark with garments shed
dance together in silver bliss.
Yours is the cup that's filled with wonder
that flows into my heartfilled sea.

Midnight's grasp and earthen womb,
leads into the world below,
where logic fails, and fear is struck
with white hot knives that pierce the flesh
to tear away the ego's burden,
that we may drink the milk of mother night.

Shining brilliance, piercing dark
Radiance of conscious power
Within my mind, Your spark exists
We speak without words
Our minds ever knowing,
and awareness ever flowing.

Coiled deep and down below
Your eyes are bright, your mouth is fire
Turning silent, writhing slow
Your primal power radiates
from deep within the land, Behold!
Awareness is your gift.

"Faery Rose Tree"
©2003

3: Stars of Magick

A Witches' Bottle

A witches' bottle is an ancient protection spell of great power. This is my version. I would recommend that anyone who is pursuing a magickal path make one to protect against any thought-forms, entities, spirits, demons, or simply negative energies that are bound to be encountered along the way. After charging, the bottle becomes an energetic trap for any force that intends to cause you harm. It is aligned to your energy-field through the use of your own DNA as well as symbolic powers that imprison and then transform harmful energy into something useful.

Items Used:
a small to medium sized jar or bottle
sage, or other purifying herb such as rosemary
a black candle
sea salt
parchment paper
dragon's blood ink
rusty nails, broken glass, needles, other sharp objects
dead bugs, some of your favorite food nicely molding, other "gross" things
some of your hair, finger or toenail clippings
some of your semen or menstrual blood
some of your urine
a handful of earth, or potting soil
a black cotton cloth

Perform this spell alone at night. On a night before the dark moon (women will need to adjust the timing to coincide with their menstrual cycle) gather your items together to perform this spell. Ground and center. Mark a circle on the ground around you with the sea salt, moving clockwise beginning and ending in the North. Burn your herb as an incense and allow the smoke to waft over you and your area. Hold the bottle over the smoke and make sure that some gets inside it. Light the black candle saying:

> *"From the darkness I conjure light*
> *from the light I summon force,*
> *from the force I invoke the power*
> *to trap that which intends me harm."*

On the parchment write the following with Dragon's Blood Ink:

Your full name
Your birthdate
Your astrological symbol for sun, moon, and ascendant
Any other symbol that you feel represents "you".

Now smear some of your semen or menstrual blood onto the paper. Draw a circle around the whole thing and draw a pentagram over it, feeling that to do so is an act of power; that when the star is completed you have erected a field of protection around you. Roll up the parchment and place inside the bottle.

Now begin to fill the bottle with the other items: your hair and clippings, nails, glass, bugs, etc. You will want to fill the bottle about halfway. Say:

> *"Insects from beneath a rock,*
> *needles, nails rusting fast,,*
> *Keep all harm inside and locked,*
> *within this dungeon made of glass."*

Now fill the jar as far as possible with your urine, which is from your body in the act of release. This will provide a link for the energy to follow into the jar and remain. Add the handful of earth, feeling it's connection to the planet and its ability to transform waste into fertility. Add three pinches of sea salt to the mixture. Cork the bottle or attach the lid and seal the edges with drippings from the black candle. Hold the bottle in both hands before you and in front of the candlelight so that the light shines through the bottle. Feel the power of the candle permeate your bottle, charging it with power and purpose. Say:

"I charge you, bottle, to trap all harm.
Keep me safe away from danger.
Inside darkness calls to darkness,
to be carried below
into the grave."

Take three deep breaths and exhale all your stress, worry, doubt fear, pain, etc. into the bottle. On the last breath "hear" the power in your breath ring and resonate with the bottle. Wrap the bottle carefully in the black cloth and open your circle in the normal way. Go outside to bury the bottle in a place where it will not be disturbed. Should the bottle ever be disturbed or broken, rest assured that the negativity will not then return to you as it has already been neutralized by the salt and the handful of earth, but the bottle will cease functioning. If you end up burying it in a place that you cannot check up on its well-being, you then may want to perform this spell at different intervals, perhaps once a year on a certain date. This of course is up to you.

Invocation of the Powers

I am talker,
I am fetch
I am Daemon
I am the Three Who Speaks as One!

I am the star who fell to earth
I am the power of the word
I am the twin and perfect flames
I am the serpent and the well!

I am the pregnant moon and waters,
I am the virile sun and trees
I am the slow yet moving mountains
I am the strong unyielding winds!

All these things and more, am I!

By stone and wind,
by flame and sea
by cobalt ring of infinity
My Triple Will made manifest!

So mote it be!
So mote it be!
So mote it be!

Invocation of the Circle

(inspired by the work and memory of Doreen Valiente, the mother of modern Witchcraft.)

By Forest dark and standing stone,
By rushing wind and life's first breath,
By flame that burns the flesh to bone,
By ancient sea, the land of death...

My blade now casts the circle round,
with razor's edge and bluest flame,
from earth to heavens, sky to ground,
the power comes that has no name.

We conjure forth the faery hounds,
From Outer Darkness now draw near,
to lurk beyond the circle's bounds,
And put invader's hearts in fear.

This holy ground now lies between
The realm of Gods and mortal men,
By human eye cannot be seen
the faery sight alive within.

Between the worlds of flesh and Fae,
we touch the Source and form the weave,
a ward to keep the worlds at bay,
that none may enter; none may leave.

As above and so below,
enveloped in a cobalt flame,
the stars that shine, the stones that know,
within we speak Her sacred name.

A Cleansing

Ground and center.

Remember how the power of the earth pulses inside of you...
in every moment;
with every heartbeat.

Remember how the wisdom of the stars sings from deep within
you... every thought, every silence, a divine gift.

Remember... and feel your power.

There it is... in the spaces between your breaths, between the words...

there S/he is...

Let Her come to you now... let Her guide you.

Light the candle. Feel it's light shine through you. It is Her light. It is
your light. It is all lights.

"Black Cauldron of the Night,
in your teeming depths are the deepest mysteries.
Let me look upon the waters
and see myself in your image."

Gazing into a bowl of water,
the candlelight reflected from your face
and breathing 3 times quick, "Ha! Ha! Ha!"
you cause your vision to awaken.

Look into the waters... look softly. There on the surface is what you
must face.

84

"Holy Daemon above me,
Descend on the light of the moon, I pray
and enter my body and flow through my souls
that I may be made pure and remember my divinity."

You hold the bowl up to your heart,
filled with water, pure and cool,
and breathe three times inside
Hearing it ring throughout the worlds.

The light of the Holy Daemon flows through you
Shining bright within your heart, it flows out and into the water.

Can you see how the water glows? Bright like fire. It sings with
power.

You drink the water in lusty gulps... drinking it down, feeling the
power...

Letting it flow through, and burn through, and change you.

Feeling the electric charge. Seeing the light fill your body. Hearing it
sing great choruses in your veins, and you joining in:

"I am pure in the light of the Holy Daemon
I am pure in the light of the Holy Daemon
I am pure in the light of the Holy Daemon
We are the Three who speak as One."

Take three deep breaths of power.

Feel this power as you breathe it through you.
In gratitude, you breathe it through you.

Give thanks to the Holy Mother.

Extinguish the candle.

Feel the silence.

Opening the Western Gate

By moon that hangs low in the sky,
By ancient sea, the earth's own womb,
I call the Gate to open wide,
That leads to life beyond the tomb.
By flesh and bone now laid to rest,
Into the earth, our Mother's breast,
By your names I here invite,
Into our circle on this night.

Protection Chant

I summon forth the strength of stone,
and conjure up these walls of rock,
Protect my soul, my flesh and bone,
My will the key, this stone the lock.

Tower of light,
Fountain of force,
Circle of purity,
Ward of infinity

Elemental Invocations

By forest tree and mountain dark,
By bone and flesh and star of north,
By our bodies, by our life,
Spirits Green I call ye forth!
From the outer darkness, I conjure earth.

By rushing wind and gentle breeze,
By rising sun where things begin,
By our thoughts and by our minds,
Spirits Yellow now come in!
From the whirlwind, I conjure air.

By warmth of fire and dancing flame,
By white-hot star and Cauldron bright,
By passion, will, and quickened blood,
The Spirits Red, I call this night!
From the eternal flames, I conjure fire.

By the rain and by the flood,
By the tide and by the moon,
By our laughter and our tears,
I summon forth the Spirits Blue,
From the watery abyss, I conjure water.

All four stars in this place be,
Combined to call the Fifth to me,
By the four made one I call ye forth,
By spirits' song I call ye in.
(OM)

Send your roots into the earth...
Then breathe the darkness silence keeps
Feeling it within your bones
Breathing in the starry deep.

Light a candle, and breathe the flame
Into the talker, cleansed by light,
Then down into the fetch's place,
To open to the Daemon's might.

By Iron's star you call your power,
Throbbing, thrumming, humming, glowing,
By star of Pearl Her blessings flower,
And brings you to the place of knowing.

Into your chalice, held to heart
full of water cool and clear
You breathe that thing which holds you back
That is your deepest, darkest fear.

The Daemon holds your greatest good,
Into the water this now flows
To charge it now with Holy Spirit
Infused with bright white fire's glow.

Drink deep this water.
Drink deep this fire.
Drink deep this power down below,
Into your belly, your fetch's point
And rocking, gently, send it now:

A smile from when your were younger.
Forgotten laughter, now relived,
And felt, thank Gods, within your flesh
The only truth to be believed.

Open now within Her light,
Flickering from the candle's flame,
The Souls of Three are now aligned
And in the darkness so remain.

Chant for a Cleansing Bath

By Salt of Sea,
I call to me,
And set in motion,
This tiny ocean,
Whose briny deep,
Shall cleanse and keep
All evil deflected,
My soul protected.

Invoking the Amethyst Pentacle

In innocence born into this world,
Drawn forth from darkness by desire.
Awakened by uncommon love
And named by self as act of power
To shine with brilliance, my own design
I sacrifice my greatest fear
And am born anew each day and night,
within this star that we hold dear.

Calling the Guardians

Hail Guardians of the East,
I summon the powers of Air!
Windswept meadow,
Breath of life,
Fantastic torrent removing strife,
With Clarity, the power to Know,
We invoke you!

Hail Guardians of the South,
I summon the powers of Fire!
Blazing flame,
Crackling fire,
The quickened pulse of heart's desire,
With Energy, the power of Will,
We invoke you!

Hail Guardians of the West,
I summon the powers of Water!
Rushing stream,
Vast, dark ocean,
Poetry of the soul in motion,
With Intuition, feeling, the power to Dare,
We invoke you!

Hail Guardians of the North,
We summon the powers of Earth!
Cave of darkness,
Standing stone,
the celebration of flesh and bone,
With Stillness, the power of silence,
We invoke you!

As above, so below.
As within, so without.
Four stars in this place be,
Combined to call the fifth to me!
Circumference and center,
Woven together,
To make the circle complete!

Spell to Ease the Pain of a Broken Heart

When love has conquered and vanquished thee
And left you ripped and torn apart
And tears and pain are all you see
Enchant this spell to ease your heart.

When night has tolled the witching hour
Gather together these objects of power:

A rose of red
Some salt of sea
A golden candle
Some chocolate candy
A chalice of water
Some sage to burn
Essential oil
An ash-pot urn

Bathe in salted water, warm
To cleanse your body and your mind
By light of candle invoke the charm
That guides you to the peace you'll find

Go then to your bedroom place
And mark a circle on the ground
And thus inscribe your sacred space
With grains of sea salt finely ground.

Waft the smoke of burning sage
Through the circle and beyond its rim
To banish hopelessness and rage
And protect all that lies within.

A pinch of ashes from the sage
Shall form a heart upon your chest
Deep and dark you fill it in
A sign of that which shall be blessed.

A golden candle you will light
In the name of Goddess Mother
And feel her flame within you grow
Your skin is shared now by another.

The chalice filled with water cool
You hold now to your heart
And praying to Her silently
Her wisdom She imparts

The water glows with crystal fire
The water glows with violet flame
The water glows with throbbing power
Elixir to cleanse away all shame.

Drink this water deep and fast
And feel the cleansing that it brings
Bask in golden candle's glow
While in your veins Her power sings.

Sitting calm and silent now
Gaze softly at the rose of red
And pluck a petal from the flower
Reciting this before your bed:

"Heart of mine that strains with sorrow
Take in the power of this spell
Begin your healing before the morrow
Let strength and honor fill you well."

Hold the petal on your heart
And then take three deep breaths of power
Then place the chocolate on your tongue
And as it melts gaze at the flower.

With scented oil, anoint your chest
Then pluck the petals that remain
And scatter them gently on your bed
So peaceful sleep you will obtain.

Say a prayer to the All-Mother
Extinguish the candle, feel the dark
Climb into bed and know beyond knowing
The healing journey has been embarked.

Healing Spell
(NOT to be used in place of professional medical care.)

Items Used:
A photograph of the person to be healed.
A green candle
A jade ring (or other green healing stone)
some red cotton thread
A drawing of the afflicted area of the body
tea tree oil
a pinch of dried lavender
a small green cloth pouch
a glass of water

Special note: If the illness has to do with cancer or another type of tumor then this will be a type of banishing and you might want to substitute black for green in this spell. Additionally you might want to use jet or onyx instead of jade.

This is best performed during a waxing moon (or waning, if it is for banishing).

Ground and center. Breathe deep and feel your power. If you work with any Gods or Goddesses that you are particularly attuned to, especially if healing is among their attributes, feel their presence now. Hold the glass of water in both hands and feel your power, and that of the Gods, flowing into and through you. Feel it flow into the water and "see" it begin to glow with the power of healing. Say something like:

> *"Healing flows into this water,*
> *flowing from Her sacred well."*

Know that the water will hold this charge until it is used. Place the cup aside for now.

Hold the candle and focus on the concept of health. You may wish to etch something on it like "<name of person> is now healed." Rub some of the tea tree oil onto it. Put it in a holder and set it aside. Do the same with the ring, placing it over the end of the candle so that it rests on it, suspended. Sprinkle some of the water around the candleholder in a clockwise circle (counter-clockwise if you are banishing).

Hold the drawing of the afflicted area. Use your feeling-sense to delve into the area of the person's body and feel the quality of energy there. If you imagine that it is too hot, for example, you may wish to imagine it cooling; if it is too active, you may try calming it down. Take the tea tree oil and draw a pentagram over the afflicted area with your fingers. Light the candle and say:

"I call forth light,
in the dark of night,
to heal the blight,
with strength and with might."

Burn the drawing from the candle flame and put the ashes in the green pouch along with a pinch of lavender. Burn some of the lavender and allow the smoke to waft over the photograph as you focus on it. See the person as surrounded by a green aura of healing (or perhaps purple, or cobalt blue for a banishing). "Feel" that they are healthy, happy, and strong. If they had a broken leg, "see" them as running on perfectly strong legs; if a problem with their lungs, see them breathing effortlessly, etc. Allow your sense of their health and newfound strength to permeate the photograph. You may wish to chant something like:

"<name of person> you are healed.
<name of person> you are strong."

You might wish to repeat this chant until you have achieved a sense of deep trance.

When you are in a deep state of trance and have felt that the healing power has been transferred to the person, then roll up the photograph and tie it with the thread. Say:

"Surrounded by a ring of jade,
encircled by the healing waters,
bound together by cord of blood,
strength restored and life renewed."

Burn the photograph, releasing the power into the universe. Mix the resulting ashes with the ashes from the drawing and place inside the green pouch. Drink the water feeling it refresh and renew you, bringing you healing energy, keeping you cleansed. Allow the candle to burn completely out. Retrieve the ring and place inside the pouch along with the ashes. Keep this hidden until the full moon (or dark moon for a banishing) at which time it should be given to the subject of this healing. If this is not possible then it should be worn by a friend or loved one as a reminder of the healing energy.

Money Spell

<u>Items Used:</u>
Green Candle
"Earthy" incense, such as sandalwood, cedar, or patchouli.
A toothpick or another sharp item to etch on a candle.

Breathe deep. Holding the candle in your hands begin to focus on your goal. "See" it as if it has already happened. Take your time with this. Allow the feeling-sense of the goal to permeate you as you will it into the candle. Imagine that the candle is now glowing and throbbing with the power of your goal. It is just waiting to be released into the universe by burning.

Place the candle in a holder and take three deep breaths. Notice the silence at the end of your breaths, how it is the primal state of being, the backdrop upon which everything else is created. Before the time of creation was the Void. Allow yourself to "tune-into" that Void now, invoking the primal state that contains all possibility. Imagine that your breath is infused with the potential that is present in all of possibility, manifest and unmanifest.

With your attention still tuned towards your goal, light the candle and say:

> *"By the light of candle bright,*
> *by the breath of dark abyss,*
> *I call abundance now to come,*
> *And revel with me now in bliss."*

Know that as the candle burns, the potential that you have placed within it is now transforming into something more real. Being transformed visibly into light and heat, and invisibly into manifestation, the energy of your goal is sent into the universe where it will plant the seeds that will sprout and grow into your magickal goal. Allow the candle to burn all the way down. If you cast a circle you may disperse it before the candle has burned out or afterwards, it is entirely up to your intuition. When the candle is burned out you may wish to keep the remains (if any) as a reminder of your rite until it is manifested. This too is up to you.

The Iron and the Pearl

From apex point of sex does flow
The gifts of love so we would know
how to find and touch our pride
where law's bright shining does abide.
Ascending into self's domain
Where all true knowledge does remain
A move towards power stirs within
Power shared with our own kin.
As waves of passion fill our souls
with wisdom to achieve our goals
By the Iron and the Pearl
I claim by being,
I claim my world.

Holy Satyr

Holy Satyr!
I invite your lust.
Horned Lord!
There is fire in your touch.
Wild God!
Ravage me and take your pleasure
Between the worlds I call your name:
Pan! Pan! Pan!
Io Evohe! Blessed be.

Storm Faerywolf is a practicing warlock, initiate, and holder of the Black Wand in the F(a)eri(e) tradition of witchcraft, which traces its lineage back to the late Victor & Cora Anderson. When he is not writing poetry, he likes to spend his time creating art, writing articles, and teaching classes on the Craft. He and his husband, Chas, have been together since 1993 and live in the beautiful San Francisco Bay Area where they run a spiritual supply store, *The Mystic Dream*. For more information about him and his work, visit his website at www.faerywolf.com

54395753R00067

Made in the USA
San Bernardino, CA
15 October 2017